WINGS

WINGS

75 tasty recipes for
fried, baked & grilled chicken

Carol Hilker

RYLAND PETERS & SMALL
LONDON • NEW YORK

Designer Paul Stradling
Editor Abi Waters
Head of Production Patricia Harrington
Creative Director Leslie Harrington
Editorial Director Julia Charles

Indexer Vanessa Bird

Published in 2024 by Ryland Peters & Small
20–21 Jockey's Fields
London WC1R 4BW
and
341 E 116th St
New York NY 10029

www.rylandpeters.com

Text © Carol Hilker 2024
Design and photographs © Ryland Peters & Small
2024

Text and images have previously been published
by Ryland Peters & Small in *Chicken Wings*
by Carol Hilker

ISBN: 978-1-78879-648-4

10 9 8 7 6 5 4 3 2 1

A CIP record for this book is available from the
British Library.
US Library of Congress Cataloging-in-Publication
data has been applied for.

Printed and bound in China.

NOTES

• Both British (Metric) and American (Imperial
ounces plus US cups) are included in these
recipes for your convenience; however, it is
important to work with one set of
measurements only and not alternate between
the two within a recipe.

• All spoon measurements are level unless
otherwise specified.

• All eggs are medium (UK) or large (US), unless
specified as large, in which case US extra-large
should be used. Uncooked or partially cooked
eggs should not be served to the very old, frail,
young children, pregnant women or those with
compromised immune systems.

• Ovens should be preheated to the specified
temperatures. We recommend using an oven
thermometer. If using a fan-assisted oven,
adjust temperatures according to the
manufacturer's instructions.

• When a recipe calls for the grated zest of citrus
fruit, buy unwaxed fruit and wash well before
using. If you can only find treated fruit, scrub
well in warm soapy water before using.

CONTENTS

INTRODUCTION

Chicken wings are a weird thing. They are one of those food trends that happened, but stayed way beyond their expected timeline. Most foods that are as coveted and celebrated as the chicken wing have been around for decades, but chicken wings have their own unique tale. They just sort of appeared one day in July of 1977 in the city of Buffalo, New York.

What started as mini-fried chicken smothered in hot sauce has now evolved into a worldwide phenomenon. Chicken wings are not just fried, but baked, smoked, grilled, double fried, slow-cooked – you name it, and it's been done (and all of these techniques are used in this book).

In the USA, chicken wings are synonymous with sports, friendship, camaraderie and the ups and downs of winning and losing. You can work up quite an appetite while watching your favourite sports team!

This book goes beyond classic chicken wings, although there are quite a selection of them in these pages. It also explores the way chicken wings are prepared and enjoyed in many different cultures, so I hope you'll enjoy sampling the delicious results.

Welcome to the world of chicken wings and other things!

1
CLASSICS

BUTTERMILK-CRUMBED WINGS

The best fried chicken always involves buttermilk, with the tangy marinade making it one of the juiciest and tastiest ways to cook chicken. This recipe is a classic.

3 eggs

500 ml/2 cups buttermilk

1.8 kg/4 lbs. chicken wings, halved at the joints, tips removed

400 g/3 cups plain/all-purpose flour

60 g/1 cup crushed saltine crackers or cornflakes

1 tsp ground black pepper

1 tsp dried thyme

¼ tsp cayenne pepper

1 tsp salt, plus extra for seasoning

½ tsp garlic powder

vegetable oil, for frying

Dijon-Blue Cheese Dipping Sauce (see page 116), to serve

SERVES 4–6

Beat the eggs and buttermilk together in a large bowl until smooth. Mix in the chicken wings, cover and refrigerate for 30 minutes.

Preheat the oven to 220°C (425°F) Gas 7. Line 2 -3 large baking sheets with foil.

Combine the flour and crackers/cornflakes with the pepper, thyme, cayenne pepper, salt and garlic powder in a large bowl.

Remove the chicken wings from the buttermilk marinade and discard the remaining marinade. Allow the excess buttermilk to drip from the wings, then press into the crumbs to coat.

Arrange the chicken wings on the baking sheets. Bake in the preheated oven for 25–35 minutes or until golden brown and the juices run clear when the thickest part is pierced to the bone. Remove from the oven.

Preheat the oil in a deep fryer set to 190°C (375°F). Fry the wings in batches for a few minutes to crisp them. Drain on a plate lined with paper towels and season to taste with salt. Serve with Dijon-Blue Cheese Dipping Sauce.

SWEET & SPICY WINGS

Honey and hot sauce – it doesn't get more Deep South than that. A little bit of sugar and a little bit of spice go a long way in this timeless dish.

1.8 kg/4 lbs. chicken wings, halved at the joint, tips discarded

350 ml/1½ cups Louisiana-style hot sauce

175 g/¾ cup butter

340 g/1 cup runny honey

pinch of garlic salt

1 tsp cayenne pepper, or to taste

salt and black pepper

Blue Cheese Dipping Sauce (see page 29), to serve

SERVES 4–6

Preheat the oven to 180°C (350°F) Gas 4. Grease the base of a large casserole or roasting dish.

Place the chicken in the dish and sprinkle with salt and pepper. Bake, uncovered, for 50–60 minutes in the oven, turning the chicken over halfway through.

Combine the hot sauce, butter, honey, garlic salt, cayenne pepper and a pinch of freshly ground black pepper in a medium saucepan. Place over a low-medium heat and melt the butter, stirring well. Increase the heat to medium-high and bring to the boil, continuing to stir, then reduce the heat to low-medium and cook for 40–45 minutes, stirring occasionally. The sauce will thicken to a syrupy consistency and will reduce by half.

When the chicken is cooked and the juices run clear when the thickest part is pierced to the bone, remove from the oven and drain off any cooking juices. Pour half the sauce into the dish and toss the chicken. Return to the oven for 5 minutes (or place under a preheated grill/broiler). To serve, pour the remaining sauce over.

Serve with Blue Cheese Dipping Sauce.

NOT YOUR DAD'S BBQ WINGS

These wings are both a little bit old school and a little bit new school! The ketchup, garlic, mustard and cayenne are pretty standard ingredients, but the addition of teriyaki and oyster and soy sauces brings an Asian twist to this otherwise classic American dish.

1.8 kg/4 lbs. chicken wings, halved at the joints, tips removed

1 small onion, finely chopped

250 ml/1 cup teriyaki sauce

250 ml/1 cup oyster sauce

120 ml/½ cup soy sauce

140 ml/½ cup Homemade Ketchup (see page 113)

4 tbsp garlic powder

120 ml/½ cup gin

2 tsp cayenne pepper

1 tsp dry mustard

200 g/1 cup brown sugar

80 g/½ cup runny honey

SERVES 4

In a large bowl, mix the onion, teriyaki sauce, oyster sauce, soy sauce, ketchup, garlic powder, gin, cayenne pepper, dry mustard and brown sugar. Place the chicken wings in the bowl, cover, and marinate in the refrigerator for 8 hours or overnight.

Preheat the grill/broiler to low.

Lightly oil the wire rack of the grill. Arrange the chicken under the grill, discarding the marinade. Grill/broil the chicken wings on one side for 20 minutes, then turn and brush with honey. Continue grilling for 25 minutes, or until cooked through and the juices run clear when the thickest part is pierced to the bone.

Tip These wings go perfectly with the Blue Cheese Dipping Sauce (see page 29).

BAKED BOURBON WINGS

This sweet and smoky sauce has a base of cooked-down bourbon as its main star. The recipe gets its name not only from the use of bourbon, but also because the dish originated on Bourbon Street in Memphis.

120 ml/½ cup soy sauce

60 ml/¼ cup vegetable oil

60 ml/¼ cup cider vinegar

60 ml/¼ cup bourbon

50 g/¼ cup brown sugar

1 tsp ground ginger

1 tbsp finely chopped garlic

½ large onion, diced

1.8 kg/4 lbs. chicken wings, halved at the joints, tips removed

Chipotle-Ranch Sauce (see page 114), to serve

SERVES 4–6

Combine the soy sauce, oil, vinegar, bourbon, brown sugar, ginger, garlic and diced onion in a bowl. Whisk until combined.

Place the chicken in a large baking dish and pour the sauce over. Toss to coat each piece of chicken with sauce. Cover the dish and marinate in the refrigerator overnight (or for at least 4 hours).

Preheat the oven to 180°C (350°F) Gas 4.

Uncover the chicken and bake for 45 minutes in the preheated oven. Turn the pieces several times during cooking to ensure they bake in the sauce on both sides.

When the chicken is cooked through and the juices run clear when the thickest part is pierced to the bone, remove from the oven. Preheat the grill/broiler to a moderate heat and place the baking dish underneath. Cook for 5–10 minutes to brown the chicken.

Serve immediately, with any extra sauce poured over. These wings are great served with Chipotle-Ranch Sauce and rice.

SMOKED CHIPOTLE WINGS

This recipe uses a smoker, then the wings are then fried and grilled, giving them a wonderfully crispy texture.

3 large handfuls hickory wood chips, divided

1.8 kg/4 lbs. chicken wings, halved at the joints, tips removed

6 tbsp Cajun seasoning

40 g/3 tbsp butter

3 tbsp finely chopped garlic

1 litre/4 cups hot sauce (such as Frank's Red Hot Sauce®)

vegetable oil, for frying

Chipotle-Sour Cream Dip (see page 125), to serve

SERVES 4–6

Preheat the smoker to 95°C (200°F) and add 1 handful of wood chips to start the smoke rolling. Coat the chicken wings with half of the Cajun seasoning. Place the wings directly on the grate in the smoker. Smoke the wings for 2 hours, adding more wood chips as necessary.

Combine the butter, garlic and remaining Cajun seasoning in a large pan over a medium heat. Cook for about 1 minute, stirring, until the butter has melted. Stir the hot sauce into the butter mixture and lower the heat, simmering for 30 minutes, stirring occasionally, until thickened.

Preheat the oil in a deep fryer set to 190°C (375°F). Preheat the grill/broiler to 190°C (375°F).

Remove the wings from the smoker and cook in the deep fryer for 5–7 minutes, until they are cooked through and are browned on the outside.

Transfer the wings to a baking sheet and coat them with the hot sauce mixture. Place the wings directly onto the wire rack of the preheated grill and cook for 2–3 minutes on each side.

Serve with Chipotle-Sour Cream Dip.

SWEET & SOUR WINGS WITH BACON

These chicken wings are a fantastic play on the Chinese take-out classic sweet and sour chicken. The wings are fried and crispy, and the salt of the bacon mixes well with the sauce. Serve with white rice for a quick, no-wait, take-out inspired dinner.

1.8 kg/4 lbs. chicken wings, halved at the joints, tips removed

450 g/1 lb. smoked streaky/American bacon rashers/slices

130 g/1 cup plain/all-purpose flour

1 tsp salt

1 tsp ground black pepper

vegetable oil, for frying

Sweet & Sour Sauce (see page 114)

.cocktail sticks/toothpicks

SERVES 4–6

Wrap each chicken wing in a bacon slice, securing it in place with a cocktail stick/toothpick.

Preheat the oil in a deep fryer set to 190°C (375°F).

Mix the flour, salt and pepper in a medium bowl and dip each bacon-wrapped wing. Coat well in the flour mixture, then shake off the excess.

Fry 3–4 wings at a time until they are a deep golden brown and the juices run clear when the thickest part is pierced to the bone. Remove the cocktail sticks.

Make the Sweet & Sour Sauce according to the recipe on page 114. Pour half the sauce over the cooked wings and serve the remainder as a dipping sauce.

BING CHERRY BBQ WINGS

Bing cherries are deep red and sweet, and their addition to this BBQ sauce turns it into something absolutely delicious. The chicken wings are fried and slathered with the sauce, but be warned – this sauce is addictive, and also makes a great accompaniment to ribs and hamburgers.

130 g/1 cup plain/all-purpose flour

1 tsp salt

1 tsp ground black pepper

1.8 kg/4 lbs. chicken wings, halved at the joints, tips removed

vegetable oil, for frying

Cherry BBQ Sauce
(see page 115)

SERVES 4–6

Make the Cherry BBQ sauce according to the recipe on page 115.

Preheat the oil in a deep fryer set to 190°C (3'/5°F).

Mix the flour, salt and pepper in a medium bowl and dip each wing. Coat well in the flour mixture, then shake off the excess.

Fry 3–4 wings at a time until they are a deep golden brown and the juices run clear when the thickest part is pierced to the bone. Toss the wings with half the sauce and serve the remainder as a dipping sauce.

Tip These wings are also great served with Ranch Dipping Sauce (see page 117).

BACON & CHEDDAR WINGS

With the addition of bacon, this might seem like meat overload, but it's really very delicious. Don't be tempted to omit the melted Cheddar sauce – once you try this recipe, you'll understand!

1.8 kg/4 lbs. chicken wings, halved at the joints, tips removed

cooking spray

¼ tsp ground black pepper

12 streaky/American bacon rashers/slices, cut in half crosswise

Cheese Sauce (see page 112)

SERVES 4–6

Preheat the oven to 220°C (425°F) Gas 7. Line two baking sheets with foil and grease with cooking spray.

Sprinkle the chicken with black pepper. Wrap each chicken piece with half a rasher/slice of bacon and place on the baking sheets. Set aside while you make the Cheese Sauce according to the recipe on page 112.

Place the chicken in the preheated oven and bake for 30 minutes, then turn the chicken over and rotate the baking sheets in the oven.

Bake for a further 20–30 minutes or until golden brown and the juices run clear when the thickest part is pierced to the bone.

Toss the wings in half the cheese sauce, reserving the remaining sauce for dipping.

2
HOT & SPICY

RED HOT BUFFALO WINGS

Frank's Red Hot Buffalo Sauce was the 'secret' ingredient used to create the original Buffalo-style wings in Buffalo, New York. It's essentially hot sauce made with cayenne pepper. This recipe has a hot base, but the use of butter gives it a slightly milder taste.

rapeseed/canola or peanut oil, for frying

1.8 kg/4 lbs. chicken wings, halved at the joints, tips removed

170 g/1 stick plus 4 tbsp butter

250 ml/1 cup hot sauce, such as Frank's Red Hot Original Cayenne Pepper Sauce®

celery and carrot sticks, to serve

BLUE CHEESE DIPPING SAUCE

150 g/1 cup crumbled blue cheese

150 g/¾ cup mayonnaise

120 ml/½ cup sour cream

SERVES 4–6

To make the Blue Cheese Dipping Sauce, place the ingredients in a medium bowl and whisk until combined. Refrigerate until ready to serve.

Preheat the oven to 100°C (200°F) Gas ¼.

Preheat the oil in a deep fryer set to 180°C (350°F).

Dry the wings thoroughly with paper towels. Working in batches, fry the wings for about 12 minutes until golden brown and the juices run clear when the thickest part is pierced to the bone. Transfer the cooked wings to a wire rack set over a baking sheet, and place in the oven to keep warm until all wings are fried.

Heat the butter in a 30-cm/12-in. deep-sided frying pan/skillet over a medium heat. Stir in the hot sauce until smooth, then add the wings and toss until completely coated. Serve the wings in a large bowl with Blue Cheese Dipping Sauce and celery and carrot sticks on the side.

DAMN HOT WINGS

vegetable oil or rapeseed/
canola oil, for frying

1.8 kg/4 lbs. chicken wings,
halved at the joints, tips
removed

115 g/1 stick butter

750 ml/3 cups hot sauce

2 tbsp chopped garlic

3 jalapeño peppers, deseeded
and chopped

2 Thai chilli/chile peppers,
deseeded and chopped

3 habanero peppers, deseeded
and chopped

2 yellow wax peppers,
deseeded and chopped

3 red chilli/chile peppers,
deseeded and chopped

salt and black pepper

SERVES 4–6

These are the hottest chicken wings in the whole book. A variety of hot peppers are used, along with a spicy hot sauce. These are not for the faint of heart!

Preheat the oil in a deep fryer set to 180°C (350°F).

Preheat the oven to 200°C (400°F) Gas 6.

Fry the wings, 3–4 at a time, turning occasionally, until golden brown. Transfer to a shallow baking dish and bake in the preheated oven for 15 minutes, turning once, or until the juices run clear when the thickest part is pierced to the bone.

Melt the butter in a medium saucepan over a medium heat. Stir in the hot sauce, garlic and peppers. Reduce the heat to medium-low and cook for 15 minutes, or until the peppers have softened. Season to taste with salt and pepper, then pour the sauce over the wings, turning to coat.

Reduce the oven temperature to 180°C (350°F) Gas 4, return the wings to the oven and bake for a further 10 minutes.

Tip These wings are great served with Blue Cheese Dipping Sauce (see page 29).

PINEAPPLE-HABANERO WINGS

125 g/½ cup crushed pineapple

120 ml/½ cup sour cream

2 tbsp habanero sauce, or other hot sauce

¼ tsp salt

vegetable oil, for frying

1.8 kg/4 lbs. chicken wings, halved at the joints, tips removed

70 g/½ cup plain/all-purpose flour

PINEAPPLE DIPPING SAUCE

225 g/1 cup plain yogurt

125 g/½ cup crushed pineapple

2 tbsp icing/confectioners' sugar

25 g/¼ cup desiccated/shredded coconut

2 tbsp coconut milk

SERVES 4–6

This recipe is a sweeter version of hot wings. However, just because it contains pineapple doesn't mean this is a dish mild on the heat. This chicken wing recipe will definitely make you sweat!

To make the Pineapple Dipping Sauce, combine all the ingredients in a serving bowl until well mixed and refrigerate until ready to serve.

Combine the crushed pineapple, sour cream, habanero sauce (or other hot sauce) and salt in a medium saucepan; whisk until smooth. Place over a low-medium heat and heat until warm.

Preheat the oil in a deep fryer set to 180°C (350°F).

Coat the chicken wings with flour by dredging them or tossing them in a bowl. Fry a few wings at a time for 10 minutes or until golden and crispy and the juices run clear when the thickest part is pierced to the bone. Toss the wings with the warm pineapple-habanero sauce. Serve with Pineapple Dipping Sauce.

YUZU PAO WINGS

This Japanese spice mixture is hot and spicy, but it's a different kind of heat than the average Buffalo hot wing heat; it's a body-cleansing heat – fragrant and delicious. But be warned – this dish will make your upper lip sweat and your eyes a little brighter!

2 tbsp coriander seeds

½ tsp cumin seeds

½ tsp ground cinnamon

½ tbsp salt

2 tbsp olive oil

1.8 kg/4 lbs. chicken wings, halved at the joints, tips removed

120 g/½ cup red yuzu pao sauce (or sriracha sauce mixed with 1 tsp yuzu juice or lemon juice)

3 tbsp runny honey

3 tbsp chopped fresh flat-leaf parsley

sugar snap peas, to serve

SERVES 4–6

Toast the coriander and cumin seeds and the cinnamon in a small, dry frying pan/skillet over a medium heat until fragrant, then let cool. Use a coffee grinder, spice grinder or pestle and mortar to grind the cooled spices to a fine powder.

Combine the spices, salt and olive oil in a large bowl. Add the wings and stir to coat, then cover and marinate in the refrigerator overnight or for at least 4 hours.

Preheat the oven to 190°C (375°F) Gas 5.

Spread the marinated wings on 2–3 baking sheets. Bake in the preheated oven for 50 minutes or until the wings are golden and the juices run clear when the thickest part is pierced to the bone. Set aside to cool slightly.

Combine the red yuzu pao sauce and the honey in a small bowl. Place the cooked wings in a large bowl, add the yuzu pao-honey mixture and half the parsley, then toss to coat. Serve hot, garnished with the remaining parsley and with sugar snap peas on the side.

RASPBERRY-JALAPEÑO WINGS

This recipe is perfect for summertime BBQs. These wings are fried and then tossed in a jalapeño-raspberry salsa-like sauce. They are sweet, but very hot, and are best served with Jalapeño-Ranch Dipping Sauce.

290 g/1 cup seedless raspberry jam/jelly

1½ tbsp runny honey

2 fresh jalapeños, deseeded (unless you want them really hot) and diced

60 g/4 tbsp butter

1 tbsp Worcestershire sauce

1.8 kg/4 lbs. chicken wings, halved at the joints, tips removed

vegetable oil, for frying

Jalapeño-Ranch Dipping Sauce (see page 117), to serve

SERVES 4–6

Combine the raspberry jam, honey and jalapeños in a small saucepan over a medium heat. Let the mixture slowly reduce to a sauce consistency, then either remove from the heat or keep warm over a very, very low heat.

Put the butter and Worcestershire sauce in a large saucepan over a medium-high heat. Once the butter has melted, add half the chicken to the pan and toss to coat. Sauté for about 5 minutes. Remove from the heat and place in a large bowl. Repeat with the remaining wings.

Preheat the oven to 200°C (400°F) Gas 6. Grease a large baking sheet with cooking spray or vegetable oil.

Preheat the oil in a deep fryer set to 180°C (350°F). Fry 3–4 wings at a time in the oil until golden and the juices run clear when the thickest part is pierced to the bone. Place all the fried wings in a bowl. Pour the raspberry-jalapeño mixture over the wings and toss to coat.

Transfer the coated wings to the prepared baking sheet and bake in the preheated oven for 5–10 minutes, until the sauce is sticky and the wings are warm to touch.

Serve with the Jalapeño-Ranch Dipping Sauce.

BROWN BUTTER & ROASTED RED PEPPER WINGS

The addition of spicy roasted red pepper creates deliciously savoury and slightly sweet chicken wings.

1.8 kg/4 lbs. chicken wings, halved at the joints, tips removed

85 g/6 tbsp butter

85 g/⅓ cup roasted red (bell) pepper, chopped

1½ tbsp brown sugar

1½ tbsp garlic powder

1½ tbsp chilli/chili powder

1½ tbsp smoked paprika

2 tsp onion powder

kosher/flaked salt and freshly ground black pepper

Roasted Red Pepper-Paprika Cream Sauce (see page 115), to serve

SERVES 4–6

Preheat the oven to 220°C (425°F) Gas 7. Line 2–3 baking sheets with foil.

Melt the butter in a large, deep saucepan over a medium-high heat until the butter browns but does not burn. Reduce the heat to low-medium and add the red (bell) pepper, brown sugar, garlic powder, chilli powder, paprika and onion powder. Season to taste with kosher/flaked salt and ground black pepper and mix well.

Remove the pan from the heat. Add half the chicken wings to the pan, stir to coat with the butter mixture, then leave to infuse for about 5 minutes. Transfer the infused wings to a prepared baking sheet, then infuse the remaining wings and add them to another prepared baking sheet.

Bake in the preheated oven for 25 minutes, turning them halfway through, until the juices run clear when the thickest part is pierced to the bone. Serve with the Roasted Red Pepper-Paprika Cream Sauce.

SPICY GRILLED ORANGE-HONEY MUSTARD WINGS

The Dijon mustard gives these wings a tangy kick, but the key ingredient is the steak sauce. This recipe is simple, delicious and proof that you don't need a lot of bells and whistles to make good food.

1.8 kg/4 lbs. chicken wings, halved at the joints, tips removed

125 g/½ cup Dijon mustard

60 g/¼ cup, plus 1 tbsp runny honey

3 tbsp mayonnaise

2 tsp steak sauce or Worcestershire sauce

zest of 1 orange

coleslaw and mini corn cobs, to serve

SERVES 4–6

Preheat the grill/broiler to medium.

Mix the mustard, honey, mayonnaise, orange zest and steak sauce together in a small bowl. Set aside a small amount of the honey-mustard sauce for basting, and dip the chicken into the remaining sauce to coat.

Lightly oil the grill rack. Grill/broil the chicken for about 20–25 minutes, turning occasionally, or until the chicken is cooked through and the juices run clear when the thickest part is pierced to the bone. Baste occasionally with the reserved sauce during the last 10 minutes.

Serve with coleslaw and mini corn cobs.

3
TRENDY

HONEY-SRIRACHA WINGS

Fried with a honey and sriracha coating, these wings are sweet and spicy. The combination mixes east and west, with a little bit of the American South thrown in for good measure.

vegetable or peanut oil, for frying

1.8 kg/4 lbs. chicken wings, halved at the joints, tips removed

225 g/1 cup unsalted butter, cut into 2.5-cm/1-in. pieces

180 g/¾ cup sriracha sauce

165 g/½ cup runny honey

1 tsp ground black pepper

2 tsp kosher/flaked salt

dash of fresh lime juice

chopped fresh flat-leaf parsley

coconut biscuits/cookies, to serve (optional)

SERVES 4–6

Preheat the oven to 110°C (200°F) Gas ¼.

Preheat the oil in a deep fryer to 180°C (350°F).

Fry the wings in batches for 10–12 minutes, until crispy and golden brown and the juices run clear when the thickest part is pierced to the bone. Remove from the oil and place on 2–3 baking sheets in the preheated oven to keep warm.

While the wings are frying, melt the butter in a medium saucepan over a low heat. Add the sriracha, honey, pepper, salt and lime juice, stirring to combine. Keep warm over a low heat. When the sauce is combined, remove the wings from the oven.

Put the cooked wings in a large mixing bowl and toss with the honey-sriracha sauce. Garnish with parsley and serve with coconut biscuits if liked.

Tip If you wish to make an accompanying Sriracha-Ranch Dipping Sauce, add 1 tablespoon of sriracha to the Ranch Dipping Sauce (see page 117).

TACO WINGS

The rich, spicy Mexican taste of these wings comes from a combination of taco seasoning, red wine vinegar and hot pepper sauce. Enjoy with a ranch dressing dip, or debone the chicken and make tacos.

1 sachet taco seasoning mix

3 tbsp rapeseed/canola oil

2 tbsp red wine vinegar

1 tsp hot pepper sauce

1.8 kg/4 lbs. chicken wings, halved at the joints, tips removed

vegetable oil, for frying (optional)

TO SERVE
Ranch Dipping Sauce
(see page 117)

Guacamole (see page 111)

tortilla chips

SERVES 4–6

Preheat the grill/broiler to medium, or heat up a barbecue grill.

Combine the taco seasoning, oil, vinegar and hot pepper sauce in a large resealable plastic bag. Add the chicken, seal the bag and shake to coat.

Grill/broil the chicken, turning occasionally, for about 15–20 minutes or until crisp and golden and the juices run clear when the thickest part is pierced to the bone. Alternatively, preheat the oil in a deep fryer set to 180°C (350°F) and fry the chicken in batches.

Serve with the Ranch Dipping Sauce, Guacamole and tortilla chips.

ASIAN CARAMEL WINGS

A sweet yet savoury sauce that brings an Asian twist to the caramel. Fried and tossed, these wings have the perfect balance of delicate flavour and sweet seasoning. Serve with Green Onion Dipping Sauce.

1.8 kg/4 lbs. chicken wings, halved at the joints, tips removed

vegetable oil, for frying

200 g/1 cup brown sugar

75 ml/⅓ cup fish sauce

75 ml/⅓ cup soy sauce

60 ml/¼ cup fresh orange juice

60 ml/¼ cup freshly squeezed lime juice

TO SERVE

egg-fried rice (optional)

Green Onion Dipping Sauce (see page 118)

SERVES 4–6

Place the sugar in a medium saucepan with 60 ml/¼ cup water over a medium-high heat and bring to a boil. Continue to boil and swirl (don't stir) for about 6–7 minutes so the sugar caramelizes evenly.

Combine the fish sauce, soy sauce, orange juice and lime juice with 60 ml/¼ cup water in a cup. Once the caramel has turned a golden amber colour, slowly pour in the mixture and return to the boil. Continue to boil for 7 minutes until the sauce is well combined, then remove the sauce from the heat and keep warm.

Meanwhile, preheat the oil in a deep fryer to 180°C (350°F).

Fry the chicken wings in batches for about 10 minutes until cooked through and the juices run clear when the thickest part is pierced to the bone. Remove and drain on paper towels. Place in a large bowl, pour the caramel sauce over the wings and toss.

Serve with egg-fried rice on the side, if using, and Green Onion Dipping Sauce.

BAKED MOJITO WASABI WINGS

These wings are an East-meets-West fusion. A mixture of a classic Mojito and wasabi produces a hot-meets-cool taste.

1.8 kg/4 lbs. chicken wings, halved at the joints, tips removed

1 tsp salt

1 tsp ground black pepper

35 g/¼ cup cornflour/cornstarch

150 ml/⅔ cup ponzu sauce

2 tbsp runny honey

60 ml/¼ cup white rum

1 tsp red chilli sauce, such as sriracha

2 tsp garlic powder

3 tbsp sesame seeds

vegetable oil, for frying

Mint-Wasabi Dipping Sauce (see page 118), to serve

SERVES 4–6

Sprinkle the chicken on all sides with salt and pepper. Dust lightly with cornflour/cornstarch and rub to coat.

Combine the ponzu, honey, rum, chilli sauce, garlic powder and 2 tablespoons of the sesame seeds in a large bowl, stirring well. Add the chicken and toss to coat. Cover the bowl and place in the refrigerator for 10 minutes.

Remove the wings from the marinade, draining the excess back into the bowl. Set the wings aside. Pour the remaining marinade into a small saucepan. Cook over a medium-high heat for 8–10 minutes, stirring frequently, and reduce until thickened and syrupy.

Preheat oil in a deep fryer to 180°C (350°F). Preheat the oven to 220°C (425°F) Gas 7. Line 2–3 baking sheets with foil.

Fry the wings in batches for about 10 minutes per batch, until the coating is golden brown and the juices run clear when the thickest part is pierced to the bone.

Arrange the fried wings on the baking sheets. Brush the on both sides with the thickened marinade. Bake for 10 minutes, then baste again with marinade and cook for 5 minutes. Sprinkle with the remaining sesame seeds and serve with the Mint-Wasabi Dipping Sauce.

DOUBLE BAKED WINGS

These crispy wings are baked until almost cooked, then coated with a Buffalo sauce and baked again. Try with Ranch Dipping Sauce or Blue Cheese Dipping Sauce (see page 117) and carrot and celery sticks.

1 tbsp garlic powder

1 tbsp onion powder

1 tsp ground black pepper

1½ tsp paprika

¼ tsp cayenne pepper

1.8 kg/4 lbs. chicken wings, halved at the joints, tips removed

40 g/3 tbsp butter

350 ml/1½ cups hot sauce or Tabasco sauce

250 g/1 cup Homemade Ketchup (see page 113)

120 ml/½ cup Ranch Seasoning (see page 117)

120 ml/½ cup soy sauce

SERVES 4–6

Preheat the oven to 200°C (400°F) Gas 6. Line 1–2 baking sheets with foil and grease lightly with cooking spray or vegetable oil.

In a large bowl, combine the garlic, onion powder, pepper, paprika and cayenne pepper. Add the wings and toss in the spice mixture.

Arrange the wings in a single layer on the lined baking sheets. Bake the wings in the preheated oven for about 30 minutes. The skin will begin to turn brown and the meat will begin to loosen from the bone.

Meanwhile, melt the butter in a medium saucepan over a low heat. Stir in the hot sauce (or Tabasco), ketchup, Ranch Seasoning and soy sauce. When the wings are done, place them in a large bowl and pour three-quarters of the sauce over them. Toss until covered.

Replace the foil on the baking sheets and rearrange the coated wings back on the sheets.

Bake the wings for a further 5–10 minutes, until the juices run clear when the thickest part is pierced to the bone. You'll have to keep an eye on them now because you will not want to overcook them. Serve with the remaining sauce drizzled over the top.

LIME & MAPLE WINGS

At first glance, you may not think that maple syrup and lime would go well together, but they are actually a harmonious combination. Fry these wings and toss them in a sticky, messy, zesty sauce.

vegetable or rapeseed/canola oil, for frying

1.8 kg/4 lbs. chicken wings, halved at the joints, tips removed

250 ml/1 cup hot sauce, such as Frank's Red Hot Sauce®

250 ml/1 cup fresh lime juice

zest of 2 limes

3½ tbsp maple syrup

75 g/5 tbsp unsalted butter, melted

2 garlic cloves, crushed

1 tsp cayenne pepper

½ tsp ground black pepper

SERVES 4–6

Preheat the oil in a deep fryer set to 180°C (350°F).

Fry the chicken wings for about 10 minutes, until cooked and the juices run clear when the thickest part is pierced to the bone. Drain on paper towels.

Meanwhile, combine the hot sauce, lime juice, lime zest, maple syrup, butter, garlic, cayenne pepper and black pepper in a large bowl. As the wings finish cooking, transfer the sauce to a medium saucepan over a medium-low heat and heat through.

Place the cooked wings in a large bowl, pour the sauce over and toss to coat. Reserve any extra sauce for dipping.

Tip These wings are also good with Ranch Dipping Sauce (see page 117).

COLA WINGS

Popular in the Southern states, these wings are basted and covered with a cola-based BBQ-style sauce.

1.8 kg/4 lbs. chicken wings, halved at the joints, tips removed

450 g/2 cups brown sugar (light or dark)

2 x 330-ml/11-oz. cans cola or root beer

3 onions, chopped

2 shallots, finely chopped

4 garlic cloves, finely chopped

4 tbsp soy sauce

¼ tsp ground black pepper

pinch of salt

2 tsp cornflour/cornstarch

Blue Cheese Dipping Sauce (see page 29), to serve

SERVES 4–6

Preheat the oven to 180°C (350°F) Gas 4.

In a medium bowl, combine the brown sugar, cola or root beer, onions, shallots, garlic, soy sauce, pepper and salt.

Place the wings in a large, deep casserole or roasting dish. Pour over the cola mixture. Bake in the preheated oven for 1½–2 hours or until the juices run clear when the thickest part is pierced to the bone. Turn the wings occasionally during cooking, to ensure they do not burn or brown too much

Remove the wings from the dish and set aside.

Pour the cola mixture into a small pan and heat. Place the cornflour/cornstarch in a small bowl, add some of the warm sauce, and mix to form a loose paste. Pour this back into the pan with the remaining sauce and cook over a low-medium heat until the sauce has thickened to the desired consistency. Toss the wings in the sauce and serve with Blue Cheese Dipping Sauce.

SPICY THAI-STYLE FRIED WINGS

This recipe is spicy, crispy and perfect for anything from picnics to family parties and get-togethers.

1.8 kg/4 lbs. chicken wings, halved at the joints, tips removed

9 garlic cloves

7.5-cm/3-in. piece of fresh ginger, peeled

6 tbsp soy sauce

6 tbsp curry paste

3 tbsp rice vinegar

2 tbsp coconut oil, melted

2 tbsp runny honey

180 g/1⅓ cups plain/all-purpose flour

2 tbsp cornflour/cornstarch

vegetable or rapeseed/canola oil, for frying

Lemongrass & Soy Dipping Sauce (see page 119), to serve

SERVES 4–6

Preheat the oil in a deep fryer to 180°C (350°F).

Chop the garlic and ginger by pulsing briefly in a food processor. Add the soy sauce, curry paste, vinegar, coconut oil and honey. Purée until smooth. Put the sauce into a bowl.

In a separate bowl, whisk the flour and cornflour with 350 ml/1⅔ cups water. Add the chicken and toss until well coated. Fry the chicken in about three batches, until golden, for 6–8 minutes until golden, then drain on paper towels.

Bring the oil back to 180°C (350°F) and fry the chicken for a further 6–8 minutes, until crisp and the juices run clear when the thickest part is pierced to the bone. Drain again, then toss the chicken in the sauce.

Serve with Lemongrass & Soy Dipping Sauce.

SAKE WINGS

1.8 kg/4 lbs. chicken wings, halved at the joints, tips removed

250 ml/1 cup soy sauce

120 ml/½ cup sake, dry sherry or dry white wine

3 tbsp very finely chopped fresh ginger

1½ tbsp finely chopped garlic

200 g/1 cup sugar

1½ tsp chilli/hot red pepper flakes

100 g/1 cup thinly sliced spring onions/scallions, (white and green parts), plus extra to garnish

3½ tbsp rice vinegar

3 tbsp cornflour/cornstarch

2 tbsp toasted sesame seeds

Plum Dipping Sauce (see page 120), to serve

SERVES 4–6

These Asian-inspired chicken wings with sake, teriyaki sauce, ginger and chilli/hot red pepper flakes are a teri-sake infusion!

In a small saucepan, whisk together the soy sauce, sake (or sherry or white wine), ginger, garlic, sugar, chilli, spring onions, vinegar and cornflour with 3 tablespoons water. Set the pan over a medium heat and bring to the boil, whisking constantly (the mixture will be very thick). Let cool. If not using immediately, cover and refrigerate for up to 4 days.

Preheat the oven to 190°C (375°F) Gas 5. Grease 2–3 baking sheets with cooking spray or vegetable oil.

Add the sauce mixture to a large bowl with the wings and mix well. Arrange the wings and sauce in a single layer on the baking sheets. Bake for 30 minutes.

Stir and turn the wings over in the sauce, then bake for a further 20 minutes. Stir and turn the wings again and bake for a final 10 minutes, or until the chicken is tender and the juices run clear when the thickest part is pierced to the bone, and the sauce is thick and shiny. Stir the wings in the sauce and transfer to a serving platter. Spoon some of the extra sauce over, then sprinkle with the sesame seeds and spring onions.

Serve with Plum Dipping Sauce.

CHOCOLATE WINGS

1.8 kg/4 lbs. chicken wings, halved at the joints, tips removed

1 tbsp vegetable oil

4 garlic cloves, chopped

2 tbsp chilli/chili powder

½ tsp ground allspice

¼ tsp ground cloves

500 ml/2 cups passata/strained tomatoes

115 g/4 oz. dark/bittersweet chocolate, coarsely chopped

1 tsp Tabasco

½ tsp salt

TO SERVE
Chocolate Ketchup (page 113)

cooked rice

spring onions/scallions and coriander/cilantro

SERVES 4–6

Chocolate and chicken might not seem an obvious partnership, but this sauce shows how it can be done.

Heat the oil in a large, heavy-based frying pan/skillet over a medium-high heat. Add the chicken wings in several batches and cook for 5 minutes, turning occasionally, until browned. Remove from the pan and set aside.

Reduce the heat under the pan to medium. Add the garlic, chilli powder, allspice and cloves and cook, stirring, for 1 minute. Stir in the tomatoes, scraping up the browned bits from the base of the pan. Add 250 ml/1 cup water, the chocolate, hot sauce and salt and cook, stirring, until the chocolate has melted.

Return the wings to the pan and lower the heat. Cover and simmer for about 25 minutes until the wings are cooked through and the juices run clear when the thickest part is pierced to the bone, and the sauce is reduced to a thick glaze.

Serve with Chocolate Ketchup and rice with chopped spring onions and coriander.

PEANUT BUTTER & JELLY WINGS

Peanut butter and jelly is probably one of the most successful and popular ingredient combinations.

240 g/2 cups plain/all-purpose flour

½ tsp salt

½ tsp ground black pepper

1.8 kg/4 lbs. chicken wings, halved at the joints, tips removed

300 g/1 cup grape jam/jelly (redcurrant jam/jelly also works well)

225 g/1 cup smooth peanut butter

2 tbsp soy sauce

2 tbsp sriracha sauce, plus extra for serving

roasted peanuts, chopped

vegetable or rapeseed/canola oil, for frying

Grape Jam/Jelly Dipping Sauce (see page 120), to serve

SERVES 4–6

In a medium bowl, combine the flour, salt and pepper. Toss the chicken wings in the seasoned flour to coat lightly. Shake off the excess.

In a small pan, combine the grape jam/jelly, peanut butter, soy sauce and sriracha sauce with 60 ml/¼ cup water. Cook over a low heat, stirring until the sauce is smooth. Keep warm until needed.

Preheat the oven to 180°C (350°F) Gas 6. Line 2–3 baking sheets with foil and grease lightly with cooking spray or vegetable oil.

Preheat the oil in a deep fryer to 180°C (350°F).

Fry the chicken wings in batches for 10–12 minutes until they are golden brown and cooked through and the juices run clear when the thickest part is pierced to the bone.

Drain the wings and transfer to a large bowl. Toss the wings with the sauce, then arrange on the baking sheets. Bake in the preheated oven for 5 minutes.

Serve the wings immediately with chopped peanuts and extra sriracha sauce on top, and Grape Jam/Jelly Dipping Sauce on the side.

4
LIGHT & AROMATIC

GREEK OLIVE & FETA WINGS

80 g/½ cup Greek olives, stoned/pitted and diced, plus a few whole olives to garnish

3 tbsp freshly squeezed lemon juice

2 tbsp olive oil

2 tbsp runny honey

1 tsp dried oregano

1 garlic clove, finely chopped

¼ tsp salt

1.8 kg/4 lbs. chicken wings, halved at the joints, tips removed

225 g/3 cups panko breadcrumbs

80 g/½ cup crumbled feta cheese

Mint-Cream Dipping Sauce (see page 122), to serve

SERVES 4–6

These chicken wings have a refreshing Mediterranean appeal. Using a mixture of breadcrumbs, Greek olives and feta, this combination of ingredietns makes a wonderfully satisfying dish.

Combine the olives, lemon juice, oil, honey, oregano, garlic and salt in a large resealable bag. Add the chicken wings, seal the bag and toss to coat. Refrigerate overnight or for at least 4 hours.

Preheat the oven to 200°C (400°F) Gas 6. Line 2–3 baking sheets with foil.

Pour the panko crumbs into a medium bowl.

Remove the wings from marinade, roll in the panko crumbs and arrange on the baking sheets. Discard the remaining marinade. Bake the wings for 35-40 minutes until golden and the juices run clear when the thickest part is pierced to the bone.

Garnish with the whole olives and the crumbled feta. Serve with Mint-Cream Dipping Sauce.

BAKED PISTACHIO WINGS

1.8 kg/4 lbs. chicken wings, halved at the joints, tips removed

2 tbsp vegetable or rapeseed/canola oil

60 g/½ cup sweet paprika

½ tsp sea salt

3 tbsp garlic powder

3 tbsp ground black pepper

3 tbsp ground ginger

3 tbsp onion powder

1 tsp dried rosemary, chopped

80 g/6 tbsp unsalted butter

1 garlic clove, finely chopped

125 g/1 cup pistachios, toasted and finely crushed

500 ml/2 cups runny honey

½ tsp sriracha sauce

Greek yogurt, for dipping

SERVES 4–6

With a sweet, honey-pistachio sauce, these wings are salty, sweet and almost healthy.

Put the wings in a large bowl, add the oil and mix together until they are thoroughly coated.

Combine the paprika, salt, garlic powder, black pepper, ginger, onion powder and rosemary in a small bowl.

Line 2–3 baking sheets with paper towels, and place a wire rack on each.

Add the spice rub to the wings and toss to coat well. Place the wings on the wire racks, cover with cling film/plastic wrap and refrigerate for 3 hours or overnight.

Preheat the oven to 225°C (425°F) Gas 7.

Remove the paper towels from the baking sheets. Keep the wings on the wire racks. Bake in the preheated oven for 20 minutes, then turn the wings over and bake for a further 10 minutes, until golden brown and the juices run clear when the thickest part is pierced to the bone.

Mix the butter, garlic, pistachios, honey and sriracha together in a small saucepan over a low heat. When warmed and combined, pour over the wings and bake for another 10 minutes.

These wings are good dipped into Greek yogurt.

BAKED PARMESAN WINGS

When baked, these wings have the taste and crispiness of fried chicken, without the decadence of fried food. They are very versatile and can be enjoyed with a variety of dipping sauces.

90 ml/⅓ cup balsamic vinegar

50 g/¼ cup salt

1 bay leaf

1 tsp dried thyme

1 tsp dried oregano

1 tsp dried rosemary

1.8 kg/4 lbs. chicken wings, halved at the joints, tips removed

7 garlic cloves, finely chopped

3 tbsp olive oil

1 tbsp ground black pepper

2 tsp chilli/hot red pepper flakes, or to taste

50 g/¼ cup fine breadcrumbs

60 g/1 cup finely grated/shredded Parmesan

Homemade Ketchup (see pages 113), to serve

SERVES 4–6

Combine the vinegar, salt, bay leaf, thyme, oregano and rosemary with 1.5 litres/6½ cups water in a large saucepan and bring to the boil. Add the chicken wings, return to the boil and cook for 15 minutes. Using a slotted spoon, transfer the wings to a cooling rack and allow to dry for 15 minutes.

Preheat the oven to 230°C (450°F) Gas 7. Line 2–3 baking sheets with foil and grease with cooking spray or vegetable oil.

Mash the garlic with a pinch of salt in a pestle and mortar until smooth. Combine the mashed garlic, olive oil, black pepper and chilli/hot red pepper flakes in a large bowl. Add the breadcrumbs, then the chicken wings and toss to coat. Sprinkle with half the cheese. Transfer to the prepared baking sheets and sprinkle with the remaining cheese.

Bake in the preheated oven for 20–25 minutes, until golden and the juices run clear when the thickest part is pierced to the bone.

Serve with Homemade Ketchup.

EXTRA-CRUNCHY CRUMBED WINGS

These wings are the perfect combination of textures – tender, soft meat enclosed in a crisp, herbed coating.

1.8 kg/4 lbs. chicken wings, halved at the joints, tips removed

500 ml/2 cups buttermilk (optional)

4 large eggs, beaten

100 g/¾ cup sesame seeds

100 g/¾ cup plain/all-purpose flour

1 tbsp coarse salt

½ tsp cayenne pepper

250 g/4 cups fresh breadcrumbs

4 garlic cloves, finely chopped

Soy-Caramel Dipping Sauce (see page 123), to serve

SERVES 4–6

If using buttermilk, put the wings and buttermilk in a medium bowl and cover. Refrigerate overnight, or for at least 4 hours.

Preheat the oven to 190°C (375°F) Gas 5. Line 2–3 baking sheets with baking parchment, or grease with oil.

Remove the wings from the buttermilk and discard. Place the wings in a large bowl, add the eggs and toss to coat.

Combine the sesame seeds, flour, salt, cayenne pepper, breadcrumbs and garlic in a small bowl. Dip each wing into the sesame mixture to fully coat. Place the coated wings side by side on the baking sheets.

Bake in the preheated oven for 30 minutes, then increase the oven temperature to 200°C (400°F) Gas 6. Cook for a further 20–30 minutes, until the wings are golden brown and sizzling, and the juices run clear when the thickest part is pierced to the bone.

Remove the wings from the baking sheets and serve with Soy-Caramel Dipping Sauce.

LEMON, BASIL & PEPPER WINGS

This might be the healthiest recipe in this book. With three primary ingredients, it's easy to mix and match and dabble with the quantities.

1.8 kg/4 lbs. chicken wings, halved at the joints, tips removed

2 tbsp ground black pepper

3 tbsp freshly squeezed lemon juice

2 tsp seasoned salt

1½ tsp smoked paprika

1 tsp garlic powder

½ tsp chilli/hot red pepper flakes

2 tbsp chopped fresh basil , plus extra to serve

4 tbsp olive oil

3 tbsp grated lemon zest, plus extra to serve

lemon wedges, to serve

Garlic-Cream Dipping Sauce (see page 121), to serve

SERVES 4–6

Combine all the ingredients except the lemon zest in a large bowl. Toss until the wings are thoroughly coated. Cover the bowl with clingfilm/plastic wrap and marinate in the refrigerator overnight (or for at least 4 hours).

Preheat the oven to 200°C (400°F) Gas 6. Line 2–3 baking sheets with foil.

Arrange the wings on the baking sheets and pour the leftover marinade over them. Bake for about 30 minutes or until the wings are golden brown on each side and the juices run clear when the thickest part is pierced to the bone.

Remove the wings from the oven and let cool briefly. Sprinkle with lemon zest and fresh basil leaves and serve with lemon wedges and Garlic-Cream Dipping Sauce.

BONELESS BAKED CHICKEN FILLETS

This is for those who don't like to deal with chicken bones – or those of you who eat pizza with a knife and fork! These 'wings' are bone-free, baked until crispy and served with a honey-chipotle sauce, although almost any sauce and marinade from this book would work well.

1.8 kg/4 lbs. chicken fillets/tenders

130 g/1 cup plain/all-purpose flour

1 tsp cayenne pepper

1 tsp garlic powder

1 tsp salt

170 g/¾ cup butter, melted

150 ml/¾ cup hot pepper sauce, such as Frank's Red Hot Sauce®

Honey-Chipotle Dipping Sauce (see page 122), to serve

SERVES 4–6

Line 2–3 baking sheets with foil, and lightly grease with cooking spray or vegetable oil.

Put the flour, cayenne pepper, garlic and salt in a resealable plastic bag and shake to mix. Add the chicken, seal the bag and toss until well coated with the flour mixture. Place the chicken on the lined baking sheets. Cover loosely with cling film/plastic wrap and place in the refrigerator for at least 1 hour.

Preheat the oven to 200°C (400°F) Gas 6.

Whisk together the melted butter and hot sauce in a small bowl. Dip the chicken into the butter mixture, then place back on the baking sheets. Bake in the preheated oven for 25–30 minutes, until the chicken is crispy on the outside and the juices run clear when the thickest part is pierced to the bone. Turn the wings over halfway during cooking so they cook evenly.

Serve with Honey-Chipotle Dipping Sauce.

GREEN TEA WINGS

60 ml/¼ cup soy sauce

3 tbsp rice wine vinegar

165 g/½ cup runny honey

2 tbsp grated fresh ginger

2 garlic cloves, finely chopped

6 spring onion/scallion greens, finely sliced

2 tbsp chilli/hot red pepper flakes

50 g/¼ cup brown sugar

10 g/¼ cup loose-leaf green tea leaves

2 star anise

12 coriander seeds

1.8 kg/4 lbs. chicken wings, halved at the joints, tips removed

TO SERVE

edamame beans

Green Tea Dipping Sauce (see page 123)

SERVES 4–6

Green tea leaves are used to spice the wings, giving an earthy hint to an otherwise Asian-inspired recipe. Green Tea Dipping Sauce makes the perfect accompaniment.

Combine all the ingredients, except the chicken and the edamame beans, in a bowl. Put two-thirds of this mixture in a large resealable bag; set aside the remaining third. Add the chicken wings to the resealable bag and toss to coat. Refrigerate overnight or for at least 4 hours.

Preheat the oven to 200°C (400°F) Gas 6. Line 2–3 baking sheets with foil.

Remove the wings from the marinade and arrange on the lined baking sheets. Discard any marinade left in the bag.

Baste the wings with the reserved marinade. Bake in the preheated oven for 35–40 minutes, re-basting the wings with remaining sauce after 20 minutes, until the juices run clear when the thickest part is pierced to the bone.

Serve with edamame and Green Tea Dipping Sauce.

STRAWBERRY BALSAMIC WINGS

These chicken wings have a deliciously sweet yet savoury, sticky taste to them. The char of the grill combines well with the strawberry and balsamic notes.

1.8 kg/4 lbs. chicken wings, halved at the joints, tips removed

450 g/2 cups strawberry jam/jelly, plus extra for brushing on the cooked wings

250 ml/1 cup freshly squeezed lemon juice

250 ml/1 cup balsamic vinegar

3½ tbsp smoked paprika

1¼ tbsp salt

French fries, to serve

SERVES 4–6

Whisk the strawberry jam/jelly, lemon juice, balsamic vinegar, paprika and salt together in a medium saucepan over a low heat. When combined, remove from the heat and let cool.

Place the chicken wings in a large resealable plastic bag and pour in the cooled sauce. Seal the bag shut, squeezing out as much air from the bag as possible. Marinate the wings in the refrigerator overnight or for at least 2 hours.

Take the chicken out of the refrigerator 30 minutes before cooking, to let it to come to room temperature.

Preheat the grill/broiler or a grill pan to medium-low heat.

Grill the chicken wings for 7–10 minutes per side, or until the wings are cooked through and the juices run clear when the thickest part is pierced to the bone. Remove the wings from the heat, and brush them on both sides with more jam/jelly. Serve immediately with a side of French fries.

BLACKBERRY & RED WINE WINGS

These wings are pure summertime. The freshness of the berries mixed with a fruity Pinot Noir give these wings a sweet taste.

780 g/6 cups blackberries (or 450 g/ 2 cups blackberry jam or preserve), plus extra for garnishing

60 g/4 tbsp butter

2 onions, finely chopped

500 ml/2 cups (or a half bottle) Pinot Noir red wine

60 ml/¼ cup freshly squeezed lemon juice

150 g/½ cup seedless blackberry jam/jelly

2 tsp ground black pepper

2 tsp salt

1.8 kg/4 lbs. chicken wings, halved at the joints, tips removed

SERVES 4–6

Put the blackberries in a food processor and purée. Push the through a fine mesh sieve/strainer into a small bowl. Set aside.

Heat the butter in a small saucepan over medium-low heat. Add the onions and sauté for 10 minutes, stirring often, until softened. Add the red wine and lemon juice. Bring to the boil; then lower the heat and simmer until reduced by about half.

Combine the blackberry pulp, jam, pepper and salt in a small bowl, then add to the wine mixture. Bring to the boil, then reduce the heat and simmer for 5 minutes. Remove from the heat, cover and cool in the refrigerator for a few hours.

Place half the sauce in a large, resealable plastic bag. Add the chicken wings to the bag and tightly seal, squeezing as much air from the bag as possible as you do so. Marinate the wings in the refrigerator overnight or for at least 2 hours.

Take the chicken out of the refrigerator 30 minutes before cooking, to let it to come to room temperature. Preheat the grill/broiler or a grill pan to a medium-low heat.

Grill the chicken wings for 7–10 minutes per side, or until the wings are cooked through and the juices run clear when the thickest part is pierced to the bone. Remove the wings from the heat, and brush them on both sides with the remaining sauce. Serve immediately.

5
TAKE OUT

TERIYAKI WINGS

350 ml/1½ cups soy sauce

300 g/1½ cups sugar

175 ml/¾ cup pineapple juice

120 ml/½ cup vegetable oil

2 garlic cloves, finely chopped

1½ tbsp finely chopped fresh ginger

1.8 kg/4 lbs. chicken wings, halved at the joints, tips removed

GREEN ONION–RANCH DIPPING SAUCE

225 ml/1 cup sour cream

225 g/1 cup mayonnaise

35 g/½ cup finely chopped spring onions/scallions

1 tbsp finely chopped fresh flat-leaf parsley

1 garlic clove, finely chopped

1 tsp Dijon mustard

SERVES 4–6

These oven-baked teriyaki wings are marinated in a tangy pineapple-based teriyaki sauce. Serve with Green Onion–Ranch Dipping Sauce.

To make the Green Onion–Ranch Dipping Sauce, combine the ingredients in a blender until smooth. Set aside until needed.

Combine the soy sauce, sugar, pineapple juice, vegetable oil, garlic and ginger in a large bowl with 350 ml/1½ cups water. Mix until the sugar has dissolved. Pour the marinade into a large resealable plastic bag. Add the wings and marinate in the refrigerator overnight or for at least 4 hours.

Preheat the oven to 180°C (350°F) Gas 5. Line 2–3 baking sheets with foil.

Remove the chicken from the marinade and arrange on the baking sheets. Brush with the remaining marinade. Bake for about 1 hour, or until the juices run clear when the thickest part is pierced to the bone.

Serve with the green onion–ranch dipping sauce

THAI GREEN CURRY WINGS

2 tbsp plain/all-purpose flour

2 tsp salt

2 tsp ground coriander

1.8 kg/4 lbs. chicken wings, halved at the joints, tips removed

vegetable oil, to drizzle

5 tbsp green chilli sauce (either hot or mild, depending on your taste)

4 tbsp unsalted butter, melted

1 tbsp fish sauce

2 tsp Thai green curry paste

3 tbsp chopped fresh coriander/cilantro, to garnish

1 fresh red chilli/chile, sliced, to garnish

Coconut Cream Dipping Sauce (see page 124), to serve

SERVES 4–6

Of all the curries, Thai green curry seems to be the most aromatic. Here, chicken wings are baked with a spicy green curry sauce that is perfect when served over rice.

Preheat the oven to 200°C (400°F) Gas 6. Line 2–3 baking sheets with foil and grease with cooking spray or vegetable oil.

In a bowl, mix the flour with the salt and ground coriander. Add the chicken and toss to coat.

Spread the chicken on the baking sheets in a single layer and sprinkle with vegetable oil. Bake in the preheated oven for 45 minutes, turning once or twice, until browned and crispy and the juices run clear when the thickest part is pierced to the bone.

In a bowl, whisk together the chilli sauce, butter, fish sauce and curry paste. Add the cooked chicken wings to the sauce and toss. Sprinkle with the chopped coriander/cilantro and serve with Coconut Cream Dipping Sauce.

GENERAL TSO'S SLOW-COOKER WINGS

Probably one of the most popular Chinese take-out dishes, General Tso's chicken has a Chinese BBQ sauce, sweetened with a combination of garlic, honey and ginger. The marinade is thick and pairs perfectly with darker chicken meat. Baked in a slow cooker, the meat falls right off the bone.

1.8 kg/4 lbs. chicken wings, halved at the joints, tips removed

5 tsp finely chopped garlic

8 tbsp runny honey

2 tsp grated fresh ginger

6 tbsp soy sauce

1 tsp crushed chilli/hot red pepper flakes

225-g/9-oz. mangetout/snow peas, cooked

a slow cooker

SERVES 4–6

Place the chicken in the slow cooker.

Mix the remaining ingredients, except the mangetout/sugar snap peas, in a bowl. Pour this mixture over the chicken and stir.

Cook on high for 3–5 hours (adjust according to your slow cooker's settings, if necessary). Add the mangetout during the final 30 minutes of cooking and stir to coat with the sauce.

Tip These wings go well with Ranch Dipping Sauce (see page 117).

KUNG PAO WINGS

120 ml/½ cup white wine

120 ml/½ cup soy sauce

4 tbsp sesame oil,

50 g/½ cup cornflour/ cornstarch, dissolved in 120 ml/½ cup water

1.8 kg/4 lbs. chicken wings, halved at the joints, tips removed

85 g/3 oz. hot chilli paste

1½ tbsp distilled white vinegar

3 tbsp brown sugar

4 spring onions/scallions, chopped, plus extra to garnish

4 garlic cloves, finely chopped

450-g/16-oz. can water chestnuts, drained and sliced

100 g/1 cup chopped peanuts

1 fresh red chilli/chile, sliced, to garnish

Soy Dipping Sauce (see page 119), to serve

SERVES 4–6

These hot and spicy Chinese chicken wings are sautéed in a pan for tender meat and a sweet and sticky sauce. Serve with rice.

Combine 4 tablespoons of the wine, 4 tablespoons of the soy sauce, 2 tablespoons of the sesame oil and 4 tablespoons of the cornflour/ cornstarch mixture in a bowl and mix together. Put the wings in a large, resealable plastic bag. Add the marinade, seal the bag and toss to coat. Place in the refrigerator to marinate overnight, or for at least 4 hours.

In a small bowl combine the remaining wine, soy sauce, oil and cornflour/cornstarch mixture with the chilli paste, vinegar and sugar. Mix together and add the chopped onion, garlic, water chestnuts and peanuts. Transfer the mixture to a medium sauté pan/skillet and heat the sauce slowly until aromatic.

Meanwhile, remove the chicken from the marinade and sauté in a second large sauté pan/skillet until meat is cooked through and the juices run clear when the thickest part is pierced to the bone.

When the sauce is aromatic, add the sautéed chicken to it and let it simmer together until the sauce thickens, then serve immediately. Garnish with the sliced chilli and spring onion.

SZECHUAN-PLUM SAUCE WINGS

This recipe combines baked wings with a spicy plum sauce. It's sweet, with an accompanying rich, deep taste.

1.8 kg/4 lbs. chicken wings, halved at the joints, tips removed

1 kg/2 lbs. purple plums, stoned/pitted and chopped

50 g/¼ cup sugar

4 tbsp hoisin sauce

3 tbsp orange zest

1 tbsp orange juice

2 tbsp soy sauce

2 tsp grated fresh ginger

½ tsp ground black pepper

Soy Dipping Sauce (see page 119), to serve

SERVES 4-6

Preheat the oven to 190°C (375°F) Gas 5. Line 2–3 baking sheets with foil.

Put the plums, sugar, hoisin sauce, orange zest, orange juice, soy sauce, ginger and pepper in a blender or food processor and blend until nearly smooth. Transfer the plum mixture to a medium saucepan. Bring to the boil, then reduce the heat. Simmer, uncovered, for about 15 minutes or until slightly thickened, stirring occasionally. When thickened, remove from the heat and divide into two. Set one half of the sauce aside.

Place the wings in a single layer on the baking sheets. Brush with the sauce, then turn them over and brush again. Bake for 25–30 minutes, turning them halfway through the cooking time and brushing with more sauce. The chicken should be thoroughly cooked and the juices run clear when the thickest part is pierced to the bone. Discard any remaining sauce that has been used for brushing the chicken.

In a small saucepan bring the remaining sauce to the boil, then transfer to a small bowl. Arrange the wings on a serving plate and serve with the warmed plum sauce and Soy Dipping Sauce.

COCONUT CURRY WINGS

These wings are fried and then tossed in a tasty coconut curry sauce. This dish goes perfectly with rice or naan bread, and makes a delicious weeknight dinner.

85 g/½ cup coconut oil

4 tsp Jamaican/Caribbean curry powder

4 tsp garlic powder

1 tsp ground ginger

generous pinch of salt and ground black pepper

1.8 kg/4 lbs. chicken wings, halved at the joints, tips removed

vegetable oil, for frying

Coconut Curry Sauce (see page 116)

1 cucumber (English) and 1 radish, chopped into chunks, to garnish

handful of coriander/cilantro, chopped, to garnish

SERVES 4–6

Combine the coconut oil, curry powder, garlic, ginger, salt and pepper together in a small saucepan and heat gently until the coconut oil has melted. Slather on the wings and put them in a large resealable plastic bag. Place in the refrigerator and marinate for at least 4 hours.

Preheat the oil in a deep fryer set to 180°C (350°F).

Preheat the oven to 200°C (400°F) Gas 6. Line 2–3 baking sheets with foil.

Fry the wings, a few at a time, in the deep fryer for 6–8 minutes until they are golden brown. Place the fried wings on the baking sheets and bake in the preheated oven for 5 minutes for extra crispness or until the juices run clear when the thickest part is pierced to the bone.

Once the wings are done, toss with Coconut Curry Sauce in a large mixing bowl. Garnish with the cucumber and radish chunks and a squeeze of lime before serving.

THAI PEANUT WINGS

These chicken wings are grilled/broiled for extra crispness and served with a warm peanut sauce.

1.8 kg/4 lbs. chicken wings, halved at the joints, tips removed

4 garlic cloves, finely chopped

225 g/1 cup smooth peanut butter

120 ml/½ cup fresh lemon juice

1 tbsp crushed chilli/hot red pepper flakes, plus extra to garnish

1½ tbsp ground cumin

kosher/flaked salt, to taste

fresh flat-leaf parsley, chopped

cucumber wedges, to serve

SERVES 4–6

Whisk together the garlic, peanut butter, lemon juice, crushed chilli/ hot red pepper flakes and ground cumin with 250 ml/1 cup warm water; season with salt.

Toss the chicken wings with 225 g/1 cup of the sauce, cover and marinate in the refrigerator overnight or for at least 2 hours.

Preheat the grill/broiler.

Grill/broil the chicken for 20–25 minutes, turning occasionally, until cooked through, lightly charred and the juices run clear when the thickest part is pierced to the bone.

Serve the wings with the remaining sauce, topped with chopped parsley and crushed chilli, accompanied by cucumber wedges.

JERK WINGS

These caramelized jerk chicken wings are spicy, juicy and very, very moreish.

1.8 kg/4 lbs. chicken wings, halved at the joints, tips removed

½ onion, chopped

35 g/½ cup spring onions/scallions, sliced

7 garlic cloves, finely chopped

4 habanero peppers, deseeded and chopped

3 tbsp chopped thyme leaves

2 tsp dried thyme

2 tbsp kosher/flaked salt

1 tbsp ground black pepper

1 tbsp ground allspice

1 tsp ground cinnamon

2 tsp ground cumin

1 tsp chilli/chili powder

1 tsp freshly grated nutmeg

4 tbsp vegetable oil

5 tbsp soy sauce

3 tbsp brown sugar

120 ml/½ cup fresh lime juice

Cajun Remoulade Dipping Sauce (see page 124), to serve

SERVES 4–6

Put the onion, spring onions/scallions, garlic, habanero peppers, fresh and dried thyme, kosher salt, black pepper, allspice, cinnamon, cumin, chilli powder, nutmeg, vegetable oil, soy sauce, brown sugar and lime juice in a blender and blend until the marinade is completely smooth. Put the chicken in a large bowl, pour the marinade over and toss to coat completely. Cover the bowl with clingfilm/plastic wrap and marinate in the refrigerator overnight or for at least 8 hours.

Preheat the oven to 230°C (450°F) Gas 8.

Line 2–3 baking sheets with foil and grease with cooking spray or vegetable oil. Place the chicken on the baking sheets, reserving the marinade left in the bowl. Bake in the preheated oven for 25 minutes.

Brush half the reserved marinade over the chicken and turn the wings over. Bake for a further 15 minutes. Turn the chicken again and brush on the remaining marinade. Bake for a further 10–15 minutes until the chicken is tender and caramelized and the juices run clear when the thickest part is pierced to the bone.

Rest the wings on the baking sheets for 5 minutes before transferring to a serving platter. Serve with the Cajun Remoulade Dipping Sauce.

CAJUN ALFREDO WINGS

These chicken wings, although very similar to the jerk recipe on the previous page, are just a smidge less hot and celebrate the fusion of the American South with Italian and French cooking. A rich Alfredo Dipping Sauce is the perfect match for these wings.

1.8 kg/4 lbs. chicken wings, halved at the joints, tips removed

2 tbsp olive oil

Alfredo Dipping Sauce (see page 125), to serve

CAJUN SPICE MIX

2 tbsp garlic powder

2 tbsp ground black pepper

1 tbsp kosher/flaked salt

1½ tbsp ground cumin

1½ tbsp onion powder

1 tsp cayenne pepper

2 tsp Italian seasoning

2 tsp smoked paprika

1½ tsp chilli/chili powder

SERVES 4–6

Coat the wings in the olive oil and set aside.

Combine all the spices for the Cajun Spice Mix in a large, resealable plastic bag and shake to mix. Add the wings to the bag, shake to coat in the spice mixture, then place in the refrigerator to marinate overnight.

Preheat the grill/broiler to medium. Line a baking sheet with foil.

Arrange the wings on the sheet and place under the grill/broiler. Grill/broil for 10 minutes on each side or until thoroughly cooked and the juices run clear when the thickest part is pierced to the bone.

Serve the wings with Alfredo Dipping Sauce.

1.8 kg/4 lbs. chicken wings, halved at the joints, tips removed

130 g/1 cup plain/all-purpose flour

4 tbsp olive oil

60 g/4 tbsp butter

1 medium onion, sliced

1 red (bell) pepper, chopped

1 yellow (bell) pepper, chopped

6 garlic cloves, finely chopped

280 g/4 cups mushrooms, chopped

475 ml/2 cups red wine

1 bay leaf

1½ tbsp dried oregano

½ tsp ground turmeric

2 x 400-g/14-oz. cans chopped tomatoes

salt and black pepper

TO SERVE (OPTIONAL)

cooked penne pasta, to serve

Parmesan cheese, grated/shredded

basil leaves

Alfredo Dipping Sauce (see page 125)

SERVES 4–6

CACCIATORE WINGS

This baked recipe combines tomatoes, peppers and Italian spices to create a beautifully rich Italian-inspired chicken wing dish.

Preheat the oven to 200°C (400°F) Gas 6.

Season the chicken wings with salt and pepper and dredge with flour, shaking off the excess.

Heat the oil and butter in a large, deep ovenproof sauté pan/skillet and fry the chicken wings on both sides. Remove the chicken from the pan/skillet.

Add the onion, peppers, garlic and mushrooms to the pan and cook for a few minutes. Add the wine, bay leaf, oregano and turmeric and cook for a couple more minutes. Add the tomatoes, stir well and cook for 5 minutes, then return the chicken to the pan. Cover the pan, place in the oven and bake for 45–60 minutes or until the juices run clear when the thickest part of the chicken is pierced to the bone.

This dish is good served over penne pasta or rice and with Alfredo Dipping Sauce on the side, if liked.

6
SAUCES & DIPS

GUACAMOLE

There is something addictive about guacamole. It is refreshing and creamy at the same time, making it the perfect match for crunchy corn or tortilla chips and also for salads, sandwiches and chicken wings!

6 avocados, peeled, stoned/pitted and mashed

juice of 2 limes

2 tsp salt

1 large onion, diced

5 tbsp chopped fresh coriander/cilantro

4 plum tomatoes, diced

2 tsp finely chopped garlic

cayenne pepper, to taste

SERVES 6–8

In a large bowl, combine and mash together the avocados, lime juice and salt. When incorporated, mix in the onion, coriander/cilantro, tomatoes and garlic. Stir in cayenne pepper to taste and add more salt if needed. Refrigerate for 1 hour before serving for the best flavour.

SALSA

This delicious salsa can be served with tortilla chips and chicken wings, or poured over crispy, baked or fried wings for a south-of-the-border flavoured snack.

3 large tomatoes, chopped

1 green (bell) pepper, chopped

1 red onion, diced

20 g/¼ cup finely chopped fresh coriander/cilantro

2 tbsp fresh lime juice

½–1 jalapeño pepper, finely chopped

½ tsp ground cumin

1 tsp kosher flaked salt

1 tsp ground black pepper

SERVES 6–8

Combine all the ingredients in a bowl. Serve immediately or cover and refrigerate until required.

SALSA VERDE

This accompaniment is tasty, spicy and hot, and goes well with guacamole.

225-g/8-oz. can of tomatillos, drained, or fresh
½ small onion, chopped
1 garlic clove, finely chopped
1 fresh green chilli/chile, finely chopped
2 tbsp chopped fresh coriander/cilantro
¼ tsp ground cumin
1 tsp salt, or to taste

SERVES 6–8

Combine all the ingredients in a saucepan with 250 ml/1 cup water. Bring to the boil over a high heat, then reduce the heat to medium-low and simmer for 10–15 minutes until the tomatillos are soft.

Purée the mixture in a blender until smooth (you may need to do this in batches). Serve immediately or cover and refrigerate until required.

CHEESE SAUCE

Use with the Bacon & Cheddar Wings on page 24.

500 ml/2 cups milk
60 g/¼ cup unsalted butter, cut into pieces
35 g/¼ cup plain/all-purpose flour
200 g/2 cups mature Cheddar cheese, grated/shredded
2 tbsp hot sauce, such as Tabasco (optional)
1 tsp cayenne pepper (optional)
salt and black pepper

SERVES 4–6

Heat the milk in a saucepan over a low-medium heat. When it starts to bubble, remove from the heat and set aside.

Put the butter in a separate saucepan and melt gently over a medium heat. Sprinkle the flour on top and whisk for 1–2 minutes until a paste forms. Remove the pan from the heat. Slowly add the warm milk to the butter/flour mixture in a steady stream, whisking until well blended. Return the pan to a medium-high heat and bring to the boil, stirring continuously, until thickened. Remove the pan from the heat, add the cheese and whisk until smooth. Stir in the hot sauce (if using), cayenne pepper (if using) and salt and pepper to taste. Cover the pan to prevent a skin forming on top and set aside. The sauce will thicken upon cooling.

HOMEMADE KETCHUP

Use with the Not Your Dad's BBQ Wings on page 15, Double Baked Wings on page 53 and Baked Parmesan Wings on page 74.

500 g/18 oz. tomato purée/paste
120 ml/½ cup white wine vinegar or apple cider vinegar
1 tsp garlic powder
1 tbsp onion powder
2 tbsp sugar
2 tbsp molasses or treacle
1 tsp sea salt
1 tsp mustard powder
⅛ tsp each of ground cinnamon, cloves, allspice and cayenne pepper
1 tsp powdered chia seeds, for thickness (optional)

SERVES 4–6

Put all the ingredients in a blender or food processor with 250 ml/1 cup water and blend well. Chill in the refrigerator overnight or for at least 2 hours

CHOCOLATE KETCHUP

Use with the Chocolate Wings on page 62.

1 quantity of Homemade Ketchup (see left)
⅛ tsp ground cinnamon
100 g/3½ oz. cooking chocolate, chopped into pieces and melted in a microwave

SERVES 4–6

Put the Homemade Ketchup in a medium saucepan over a medium heat and bring to a simmer. When the mixture has been warmed thoroughly, stir in the cinnamon and melted chocolate. When well mixed together, remove from the pan and refrigerate before serving.

CHIPOTLE–RANCH SAUCE

Use with the Baked Bourbon Wings on page 16.

225 g/1 cup light mayonnaise
250 ml/1 cup sour cream
3 tbsp Ranch Seasoning (see page 117)
3 spring onions/scallions, finely chopped
1 garlic clove, finely chopped
1 canned chipotle chilli/chile, finely chopped
1 tbsp fresh lime juice

SERVES 4–6

Put all the ingredients in a bowl and whisk until thoroughly combined.

SWEET & SOUR SAUCE

Use with the Sweet & Sour Wings with Bacon on page 20.

150 g/¾ cup white sugar
75 ml/⅓ cup white wine vinegar
60 ml/¼ cup soy sauce
1 tbsp Homemade Ketchup (see page 113)
2 tbsp cornflour/ cornstarch
150 ml/⅔ cup water
125 g/½ cup chopped pineapple

SERVES 4–6

Combine the sugar, vinegar, soy sauce and ketchup in a medium saucepan. In a bowl, blend the cornflour/ cornstarch with 2 tablespoons of the water and mix together until smooth. Stir in the remaining water and pineapple, then pour the mixture into the saucepan. Bring to the boil, stirring well, then reduce the heat and simmer until the sauce has thickened.

CHERRY BBQ SAUCE

Use with the Bing Cherry BBQ Wings on page 23.

2 tbsp butter

1 onion, chopped

3 garlic cloves, finely chopped

400 g/2 cups fresh or frozen Bing cherries (or other dark, sweet cherries), stoned/pitted and coarsely chopped

250 g/1 cup Homemade Ketchup (see page 113)

130 g/⅔ cup packed brown sugar

60 ml/¼ cup cider vinegar

1 tbsp Worcestershire sauce

2 tsp mustard powder

½ tsp ground black pepper

SERVES 4–6

Melt the butter in a large saucepan, add the onion and sauté until tender. Add the garlic and continue to cook for 1 minute. Stir in the remaining sauce ingredients. Cook, uncovered, over a medium-low heat for 20 minutes or until the cherries are tender and the sauce has thickened, stirring occasionally. Set aside and let cool.

ROASTED RED PEPPER -PAPRIKA CREAM SAUCE

Use with the Brown Butter & Roasted Red Pepper Wings on page 38.

85 g/⅓ cup roasted red (bell) pepper, chopped

60 g/¼ cup goat's cheese

2 tbsp sour cream

1 tbsp paprika

¼ tsp salt

SERVES 4–6

Mix all the ingredients in a blender until thoroughly combined and smooth. Refrigerate until ready to serve.

COCONUT CURRY SAUCE

Use with the Coconut Curry Wings on page 98.

2 tbsp coconut oil

1 garlic clove, crushed and finely chopped

2 tbsp freshly grated ginger

2 tbsp Jamaican/Caribbean curry powder

1 tsp crushed chilli/hot red pepper flakes

400 ml/1¾ cups coconut milk

3 tbsp runny honey

2 tbsp soy sauce

freshly squeezed juice of 2 limes, plus a squeeze for serving

couple of pinches of nutmeg

SERVES 4–6

Combine the coconut oil with the garlic, ginger, curry powder and chilli/hot red pepper flakes in a medium saucepan and cook gently for 2 minutes. Add the coconut milk, honey, soy sauce, lime juice and nutmeg. Bring to a light simmer and let it reduce for 40–45 minutes until it reaches a thicker consistency.

DIJON-BLUE CHEESE DIPPING SAUCE

Use with the Buttermilk-Crumbed Wings on page 11.

100 ml/½ cup mayonnaise

120 ml/½ cup sour cream

2 tsp fresh lemon juice

2 tsp red wine vinegar

1 tsp creamy Dijon mustard

¼ tsp Worcestershire sauce

50 g/⅓ cup crumbled blue cheese

1 garlic clove, finely chopped

1–2 tbsp chopped fresh flat-leaf parsley

1 spring onion/scallion, finely chopped

salt and black pepper

SERVES 4

Stir or whisk the mayonnaise, sour cream, lemon juice, vinegar, mustard and Worcestershire sauce in a bowl until smooth. Add the blue cheese, garlic, parsley and spring onion/scallion, and stir until combined. Season to taste, then cover and refrigerate for at least 1 hour before serving.

RANCH DIPPING SAUCE

Use with the Bing Cherry BBQ Wings on page 23, Taco Wings on page 46, Lime & Maple Wings on page 54 and General Tso's Slow-Cooker Wings on page 93.

75 g/⅓ cup mayonnaise or Greek yogurt

75 ml/⅓ cup milk

1 tsp hot sauce or sriracha (optional)

RANCH SEASONING

35 g/⅓ cup dried buttermilk or powdered milk

2 tbsp dried parsley

1½ tsp dried dill

2 tsp garlic powder

2 tsp onion powder

2 tsp dried onion flakes

1 tsp ground black pepper

1 tsp dried chives

1 tsp salt

SERVES 4–6

Combine the ranch seasoning in a bowl. Put the mayonnaise or yogurt, milk and 1 tablespoon of the ranch seasoning in a small bowl and whisk to combine. Add the hot sauce for a Hot Pepper Ranch Dipping Sauce.

Note: 3 tablespoons of this ranch seasoning is the same as 1 packet of store-bought seasoning. Any unused seasoning can be stored in an airtight container.

JALAPEÑO–RANCH DIPPING SAUCE

Use with the Raspberry-Jalapeño Wings on page 37.

300 g/1⅓ cups mayonnaise

90 ml/⅓ cup buttermilk

90 ml/⅓ cup Salsa Verde (see page 112)

3 tbsp chopped canned green chillies/chiles

2 jalapeño peppers, halved and deseeded

3 tbsp Ranch Seasoning (see opposite)

SERVES 4–6

Put all the ingredients into a blender and process until smooth. Chill before serving.

MINT-WASABI DIPPING SAUCE

Use with the Baked Mojito Wasabi Wings on page 50.

175 ml/¾ cup Greek yogurt
¼ tsp wasabi powder
2 tbsp finely chopped coriander/cilantro
1 tbsp fresh lime juice
2 fresh mint leaves, finely chopped

SERVES 4–6

Combine all the ingredients in a small bowl and chill before serving.

GREEN ONION DIPPING SAUCE

Use with the Asian Caramel Wings on page 49.

250 ml/1 cup sour cream
225 g/1 cup mayonnaise
50 g/½ cup finely chopped spring onions/scallions
30 g/½ cup finely chopped fresh flat-leaf parsley
2 garlic cloves, finely chopped
1 tsp Dijon mustard

SERVES 4–6

Mix all the ingredients together in a blender until smooth. Refrigerate before serving.

SOY DIPPING SAUCE

Use with the Kung Pao Wings on page 94 and Szechuan-Plum Sauce Wings on page 97.

60 ml/¼ cup soy sauce
60 ml/¼ cup sour cream
1 tbsp rice wine vinegar
1 tbsp finely sliced spring onions/scallions

SERVES 4–6

Combine all the ingredients in a blender or food processor, then chill in the refrigerator before serving.

LEMONGRASS & SOY DIPPING SAUCE

Use with the Spicy Thai-style Fried Wings on page 58.

3 stalks of lemongrass
2 spring onions/scallions, chopped
1 tsp finely chopped garlic
1 tsp brown sugar
1 tbsp sriracha sauce
3 tbsp fresh lime juice
1 tbsp fish sauce
2 tsp soy sauce
1 tbsp chopped fresh coriander/cilantro
1 tbsp chopped fresh basil

SERVES 4–6

Trim the ends of the lemongrass stalks and remove the outer layers, then finely chop. Place in a bowl with the other ingredients and 3 tablespoons water. Mix well, then chill in the refrigerator before serving.

PLUM DIPPING SAUCE

Use with the Sake Wings on page 61.

1.3 kg/3 lbs. plums, pitted and chopped
4 garlic cloves, finely chopped
1 tbsp finely chopped fresh ginger
1 small onion, finely chopped
200 g/1 cup brown sugar
2 tbsp teriyaki sauce
1 tsp sesame oil
2 tbsp soy sauce
½ tsp crushed dried chilli
juice of 1 lemon
2 tbsp cornflour/cornstarch

SERVES 4–6

Put all the ingredients except the cornflour/
cornstarch in a medium saucepan with
475 ml/2 cups water. Bring to the boil, then
reduce the heat and simmer for 30 minutes.
Remove from the heat.

Mix the cornflour with 1 tablespoon water,
then pour into a blender with the plum
mixture. Blend until combined. Pour back
into the pan and cook over a medium-low
heat until the mixture thickens to the desired
consistency.

GRAPE JELLY/JAM DIPPING SAUCE

Use with the Peanut Butter & Jelly
Wings on page 65.

150 g/½ cup grape jelly/jam
150 g/½ cup plain or vanilla yogurt

SERVES 4–6

Heat the jelly/jam in a small saucepan
over a low heat. When it is smooth, mix
the warmed jelly with the yogurt. Serve
immediately.

PIZZA DIPPING SAUCE

Use with the Baked Parmesan Wings on page 73.

250 ml/1 cup passata/strained tomatoes
1 tbsp Italian seasoning
2 tsp dried oregano
1 tsp garlic powder

SERVES 4–6

Simmer the passata in a saucepan with all the seasonings for about 20 minutes, then leave to cool.

GARLIC-CREAM DIPPING SAUCE

Use with the Lemon, Basil & Pepper Wings on page 77.

120 g/½ cup plain yogurt
120 ml/½ cup sour cream
100 g/½ cup mayonnaise
8 garlic cloves, or to taste, finely chopped
¼ tsp paprika
½ tsp salt
¼ tsp ground black pepper
fresh chives, finely chopped

SERVES 4–6

Mix all the ingredients except the chives together until smooth and well combined. Chill until ready to serve, then garnish with the chives.

MINT-CREAM DIPPING SAUCE

Use with the Greek Olive & Feta Wings on page 69.

250 g/1 cup plain Greek yogurt

juice of 1 lime

3 garlic cloves, crushed

30 g/1 cup fresh mint leaves, finely chopped, plus extra to garnish

¼ tsp cayenne pepper

1 tsp ground cumin

1 tsp paprika

1 tsp ground coriander

salt

SERVES 4–6

Mix all the ingredients together in a bowl until smooth and creamy.

HONEY-CHIPOTLE DIPPING SAUCE

Use with the Boneless Baked Chicken Fillets on page 78.

340 g/1¼ cups runny honey

120 ml/½ cup tomato ketchup (or Homemade Ketchup, see page 113)

1½ tbsp white wine vinegar

1 tbsp ground chipotle chilli powder

¾ tsp salt

SERVES 4–6

Combine all the ingredients in a medium saucepan with 120 ml/½ cup water and bring to the boil over a medium-high heat. Reduce the heat once the mixture comes to the boil and let simmer for 3–5 minutes.

SOY-CARAMEL DIPPING SAUCE

Use with the Extra-Crunchy Crumbed Wings on page 74.

75 g/⅓ cup sugar

4–5 large shallots, chopped

1 garlic clove, finely chopped

½ tbsp finely chopped fresh ginger

3 tbsp soy sauce

3 tbsp rice vinegar (not seasoned)

2 tbsp cornflour/cornstarch

1 tbsp fresh lemon juice (optional)

SERVES 4–6

Cook the sugar in a large, dry, heavy-based saucepan over a medium-high heat, undisturbed, until it melts around edges and begins to turn a perfect golden colour.

Add the shallots (use caution as the caramel will bubble up and steam vigorously) and cook for about 45 seconds, stirring, until the shallots shrink and become fragrant. Add the garlic and ginger and cook, stirring, for 30 seconds. Stir in the soy sauce, vinegar and 335 ml/1⅓ cups water and simmer for 1 minute, stirring, until any hardened caramel has dissolved. The sauce will turn a rich auburn colour.

Mix the cornflour with 2 tablespoons water until smooth, then stir into the sauce and simmer for 2 minutes, stirring occasionally. Remove from the heat and plunge the pan into a sink of cold water to stop the caramel cooking. If using lemon juice, stir it in now. Cover the sauce and keep warm.

GREEN TEA DIPPING SAUCE

Use with the Green Tea Wings on page 81.

300 ml/1¼ cups sour cream

1 tbsp loose-leaf green tea

1 spring onion/scallion, finely chopped (green parts only)

SERVES 4–6

Combine the sour cream and green tea leaves in a small bowl, then set aside for 1 hour. Add the spring onion/scallion just before serving.

COCONUT CREAM DIPPING SAUCE

Use with the Thai Green Curry Wings on page 90.

400-g/16-oz. can coconut milk
225 g/1 cup brown sugar

SERVES 4–6

Combine the ingredients in a medium saucepan and bring to the boil over a medium-high heat. Reduce the heat to medium-low and cook, stirring, for about 20 minutes until the mixture is thick and the volume has reduced by about half.

CAJUN REMOULADE DIPPING SAUCE

Use with the Jerk Wings on page 102.

500 g/2 cups mayonnaise
2 tbsp Homemade Ketchup (see page 113)
2 tbsp English mustard
1 tbsp chopped fresh flat-leaf parsley
1 tbsp cayenne pepper
1 tbsp fresh lemon juice
2 tsp prepared horseradish
3 garlic cloves, finely chopped
1 tsp Worcestershire sauce
1 tsp celery salt
1 tsp paprika

SERVES 4–6

Combine all ingredients in a blender or food processor. Refrigerate before serving.

ALFREDO DIPPING SAUCE

Use with the Cajun Alfredo Wings on page 105 and Cacciatore Wings on page 106.

2 tbsp olive oil
60 g/4 tbsp butter
4 garlic cloves, finely chopped
850 ml/4 cups whipping cream
½ tsp ground black pepper
75 g/1 cup grated/shredded Parmesan cheese
200 g/ 1½ cups grated/shredded mozzarella

SERVES 4–6

In a medium saucepan over a medium heat, combine the olive oil with the butter and garlic and cook until the garlic becomes aromatic. Add the cream and pepper and bring to a simmer, stirring often. Let the sauce thicken to desired consistency – this will take 30–40 minutes. Remove from the heat and stir in the cheese.

CHIPOTLE-SOUR CREAM DIP

Use with the Smoked Chipotle Wings on page 19.

210-g/7-oz. can chipotle chillies/chiles in adobo sauce
450 ml/2 cups sour cream
1 tbsp ground cumin
juice of 1 lime
salt

SERVES 4–6

Put the chillies in a blender with the sour cream, cumin, lime juice and a few good pinches of salt. Pulse in the blender until well combined. Refrigerate for at least 2 hours before serving.

INDEX

ACKNOWLEDGEMENTS

I would like to thank my friends and family for their love and support, and for their senses of humour. I have great friends and i am so very blessed for that.

Most importantly, I would like to thank the rest of the team behind this book. The talented Toby Scott did a simply stunning job and special thanks go to Leslie Harrington, Maria Lee-Warren, Rosie Reynolds, Luis Peral, and finally to Nathan Joyce, an editor extraordinaire with the patience of a saint. These people are beyond talented at what they do and I am humbled to be able to collaborate with them.

I would also like to thank Julia Charlies and Cindy Richards for allowing me to work with such a great team on such fantastic projects. Go chicken wings!

ABOUT THE AUTHOR

Carol Hilker is a full-time food writer based in San Francisco. She trained and worked as a pastry chef and has since forged a successful career as a cookbook author. She wrote the hugely popular *Dirty Food*, as well as *Pie Pops* and *Mmm… Marshmallows* for Ryland Peters & Small.